MEIA

CAR BOOT
GENIE

Jillian Powell

Illustrated by Anthony Williams

First Fli

D1324700

Titles in First Flight

Badger Publishing Limited
15 Wedgwood Gate, Pin Green Industrial Estate,
Stevenage, Hertfordshire SG1 4SU
Telephone: 01438 356907. Fax: 01438 747015
www.badger-publishing.co.uk
enquiries@badger-publishing.co.uk

Car Boot Genie ISBN 978 1 84424 835 3

Series Editor: Jonny Zucker
Publisher: David Jamieson
Commissioning Editor: Carrie Lewis
Editor: Paul Martin
Design: Fiona Grant
Illustration: Anthony Williams

CAR BOOT GENIE

Jillian Powell

Contents

Something shiny

"How much have we made?"
Ryan asked.

Pritesh counted out the money.

"Twenty-one pounds and fifty pence."

"Fifty pence?"

"I just sold that computer game,"
Pritesh said. "The one with the
car chase."

"Well, I told Mum we'd sell all our stuff," Ryan said.

"Yeah," Pritesh agreed. "And we've made ten pounds each."

"Um, ten pounds and seventy-five pence!" Ryan said.

Pritesh handed over the money. "Time to pack up then?"

The boys started packing up.

"If we are quick, we will be in time for the match," Ryan said.

Their school team was playing at home in a big match.

"Hey, see that?"

Ryan was pointing at an old teapot.

"Yes! Gross or what?" Pritesh said.

"Yeah, but my Nan would love that!" Ryan said.

"It's just the sort of gold stuff she goes for."

"How much for this?" he asked the man behind the table.

The man picked up the teapot.
It glinted in the sunshine.

"One pound fifty," the man said.

"Done!" Ryan said.

"You have been done, mate,"
Pritesh said.

The goal that wasn't

The match had started when they got there. It was one-all.

"Put that teapot down," Pritesh said to Ryan.

"I don't want to break it," Ryan said.

"I would," Pritesh said. "It's horrible."

"But it's gold and it makes tea. Nan will love it," Ryan said.

"Okay, okay," Pritesh said.
He liked Ryan's Nan.
She made lush cakes.

"What's he doing? He's off-side!"

Ryan jumped up and down.
The ball was near their goal.

"It's an open goal. We're done for!"
Pritesh said.

"No, Scott's there. He'll head it away...
No...o! I don't believe it!"

Scott Betts had scored an own goal.
The other team was dancing up
and down.

"Oh Bettsy. I wish you hadn't done that!"
Ryan groaned.

Then something odd happened. It was
like seeing a video re-wind. The ball
came back out of the net. It hit
Scott Betts' head. Then it went
back down the pitch.

The other team stopped dancing. It was
one-all again.

"Did you see that?" Pritesh blinked.

"I think I'm dreaming," Ryan said.

"In fact I know I am now."

Their team had just scored: this time it
was in the right goal.

"That was a result!" Pritesh said as they got on the bus home.

"I still don't get it," Ryan said.

"I wish this bus would hurry up," Pritesh said.

"I want to have a go on the Xbox. I think I can get to level five."

"Five?" Ryan asked. "You mean you are only at…"

There was no time to say any more. Suddenly, the bus overtook a sports car, then a police car!

"What is he playing at?" Ryan was fighting to stay in his seat - and hold on to the teapot.

Very soon the brakes screamed. They had reached their home stop.

They got out. Their legs felt like jelly.

"Well you said you wanted him to hurry up," Ryan said.

The bus pulled out. It was going as fast as a milk float.

"Well, at least the teapot is okay," Ryan said.

Pritesh shook his head. Had everyone gone mad around here?

"Are you really only on level five?"
Ryan asked Pritesh.

"Yeah, well. I could get to six easily,"
Pritesh said. "If only we didn't have
this rubbish maths test to do."

"I know. Trust Mr Simms to give us the
maths test tonight," Ryan said. "I wish
he hadn't."

"Is that your phone ringing?"
Pritesh asked.

"Hello?" Ryan said.

"Hello, Ryan." It was their maths
teacher, Mr Simms.

"Mr Simms?" Ryan was worried.
What had he done wrong now?

"I just wanted to say, don't do the maths test tonight," Mr Simms said. "I gave you the wrong papers."

"Don't do the maths test...?" Ryan said again, so Pritesh could hear.

"What?" Pritesh gasped.

"That's all, Ryan. See you in school tomorrow."

"Yes, thanks Mr Simms. See you there!" Ryan rang off.

"Can you believe that?" he asked Pritesh.

But Pritesh was staring at the teapot.

There was thick yellow smoke coming out of it.

The genie

"What a stink!" Pritesh said.

"It will set the smoke alarm off!" Ryan said. "I'd better wash it out."

There wasn't time. Soon the room was full of smoke. And there was a strange noise like water going down a plug hole.

The smoke hung in a cloud. Then a giant gold man stepped out of it.

"I am a genie," he roared.

"A…a genie? You mean like a genie of the…teapot?" Ryan said.

"Yes, Master."

The genie folded his arms. He looked as if he was waiting for something.

Ryan looked at Pritesh.

"Is it like…I mean, do we get to make three wishes or something?"

"Yes, Master. You did," the genie said with a smile.

"We did?"

"Yes, Master."

"Oh, I get it." Pritesh said slowly. "The football match…and the bus ride…"

"And the maths test," Ryan added.

"Yes, Master."

"But that's not fair!" the boys said together. "I mean, we didn't know we were making wishes."

"You wished three times, Master," the genie replied.

"Oh, we've messed up big time!"
Pritesh said to Ryan. "We could have
wished for anything!"

"What about my Nan?" Ryan asked
the genie. "The teapot is hers really."

"Your Nan?" The genie smiled.
"You can make a wish for your Nan."

Ryan thought hard.

"Okay. I wish Nan's leg was better," he said.

The genie nodded and smiled. Then he vanished.

"So your leg really is better then, Nan?" Ryan asked.

"Yes. I walked to the shops, no problem!" Nan replied.

"And that's not all. I found my glasses, those ones I'd lost. I was so pleased."

"I know you kept wishing you could find them," Ryan said. He looked at Pritesh.

"Now then, what do we have here?"
Nan asked.

"It's a present," Ryan said. "I hope you
like it."

He gave Nan the teapot.

"Oh Ryan, it's lovely!" Nan said, holding up the pot. Ryan gave Pritesh a look that said "I told you so!"

"How about a nice cup of tea!" Nan said. "I've made a chocolate cake."

"Lush!" Pritesh said.

"Put the kettle on please, Ryan."

"Okay Nan. Um, which teapot
shall I use?"

Nan was still holding the gold teapot.
Ryan nudged Pritesh. There was yellow
smoke coming out of it.

A third wish

"I don't want to break your new pot, "
Ryan said to Nan.

"Oh, use the old one, Ryan. I'll keep
this one for show!" Nan said.

"Phew!" Ryan said to Pritesh in the
kitchen. "I don't think that genie bloke
would like teabags in his face!"

They took the tea and cake through
to Nan.

"You are good boys," Nan said. "You know what I wish?"

"What's that Nan?"

Ryan was watching the teapot.

"I wish I could win that lottery so I could really treat you both."

Just then, there was a ring at the doorbell.

"Now who's that?" Nan said.

Ryan looked at Pritesh.

"Mrs Walker?" They heard a man say. "I have some very good news for you."